ONCE UPON A TIME IN CHINA

THE GREATEST EXPLORER IN THE WORLD

JILLIAN LIN

Illustrations by SHI MENG

Zheng He (1371–1433), world explorer, Ming Dynasty

Once upon a time in China…

… the Chinese had the biggest fleet of ships in the world. Some of these were the largest ships ever built at the time. One ship was as long as a football field.

The large ships were loaded with treasure, carrying the best teas, porcelains, silks, and other special goods from China.

China
Asia
Iran
Nanjing
Fuzhou
Hulumosi
Keelung
Arab
Bengal
India
Mecca
Champa
Kori
Siam
Africa
Sri Lanka
Malacca
Yemen
Somalia
Sumatra
Kenya
Java

Some ships held only horses and others carried fresh water. There were also war ships full of weapons and supply ships carrying food, medicines, and everything else the sailors needed.

At the head of the fleet was Admiral Zheng He (*Jeung Huh*). This is the story of how he became the commander of the Chinese fleet.

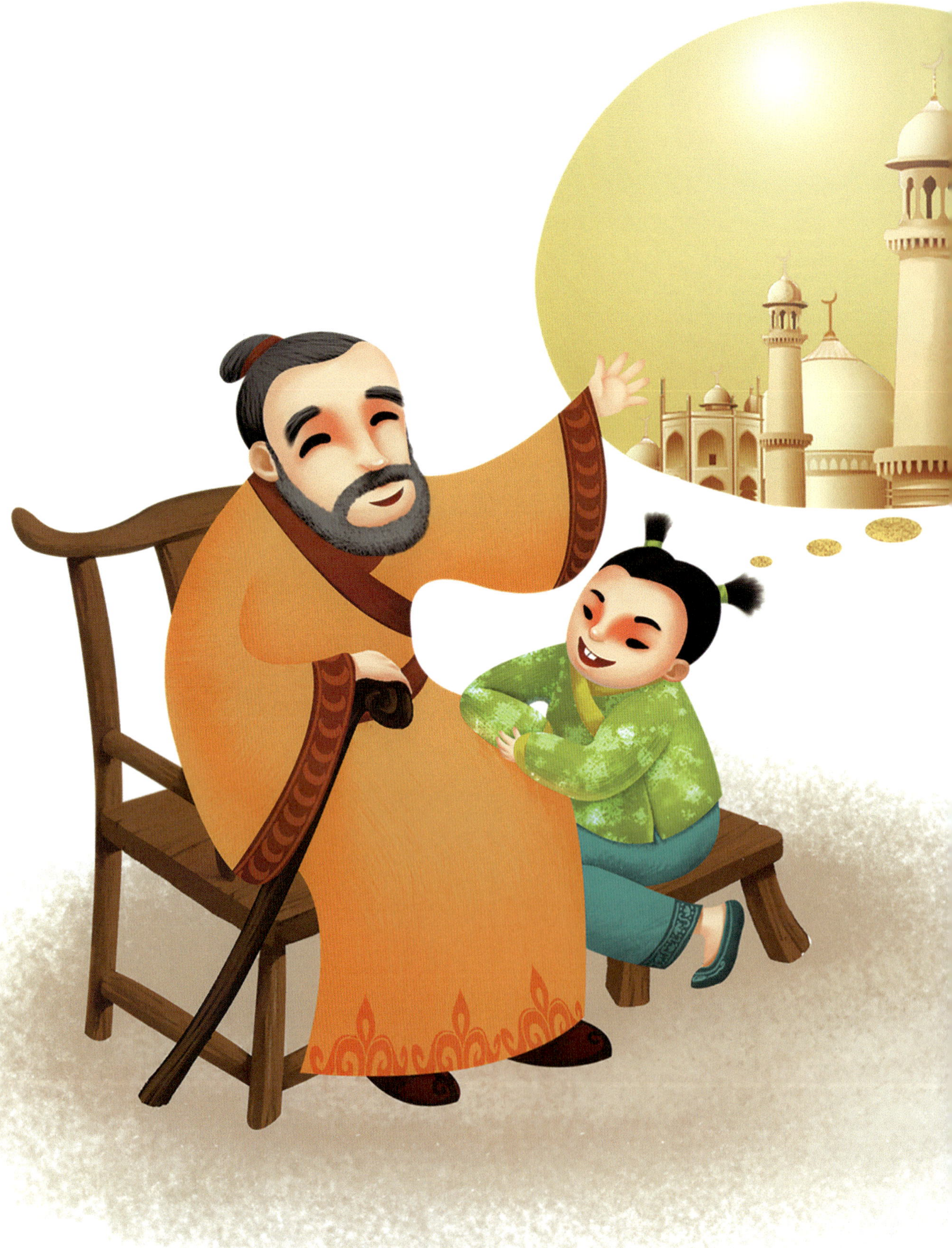

Zheng He grew up in the mountains south of China, but he was not Chinese. He was raised in a family of Muslims.

As a little boy he always loved listening to his father's and grandfather's stories about their journeys to the holy city of Mecca. He would daydream about how he would travel to these strange and faraway lands one day.

When Zheng He was ten years old, his life changed forever. At that time, the Mongols from the north ruled most of China. Zheng He's father and grandfather were leaders for the Mongols.

One day, an army of soldiers attacked his home town. The army belonged to a new Chinese emperor.

The emperor tried to take over from the Mongols so China would be in the hands of the Chinese again.

In Zheng He's town, the Mongols fought hard against the army, but in the end, they lost the battle.

The Chinese soldiers took Zheng He away from his family and sent him to a palace in Beijing.

Of course, Zheng He was sad to be taken away from home. But luckily, he was a clever and strong-minded boy so he decided to work hard at the palace. He learned to read and write, and became a servant for Prince Zhu Di, one of the Chinese emperor's 26 sons.

Zheng He grew up to become a tall and heavily built man with a clear and loud voice. He was also a brave soldier. As a leader in the army, he helped the prince become the new emperor of China.

The emperor told Zheng He, 'Thank you for all your help, my friend. I would like you to sail across the seas and show the whole world what a great country China is.'

Zheng He was excited. This was his chance to see his childhood dream come true – to visit and explore faraway lands. Immediately, he ordered the building of many ships until hundreds of them were ready to launch.

As the leader of the fleet, Zheng He had more than 25,000 people under his command: navigators to read maps and use the compass, meteorologists to predict the weather and technicians to do ship repairs, as well as doctors, cooks, translators, and sailors.

Now he was ready for his very first sea voyage.

The fleet of ships visited countries along the Indian Ocean like Vietnam, Malaysia, and Indonesia. They got as far as India.

In most places they received a warm welcome. Zheng He told the leaders of the foreign lands, 'Please accept these treasures from our homeland. The emperor of China would like our countries to become friends.'

That is how Zheng He started to exchange Chinese treasures like porcelain and silk with special goods like gems, stones, spices, ivory, and pearls.

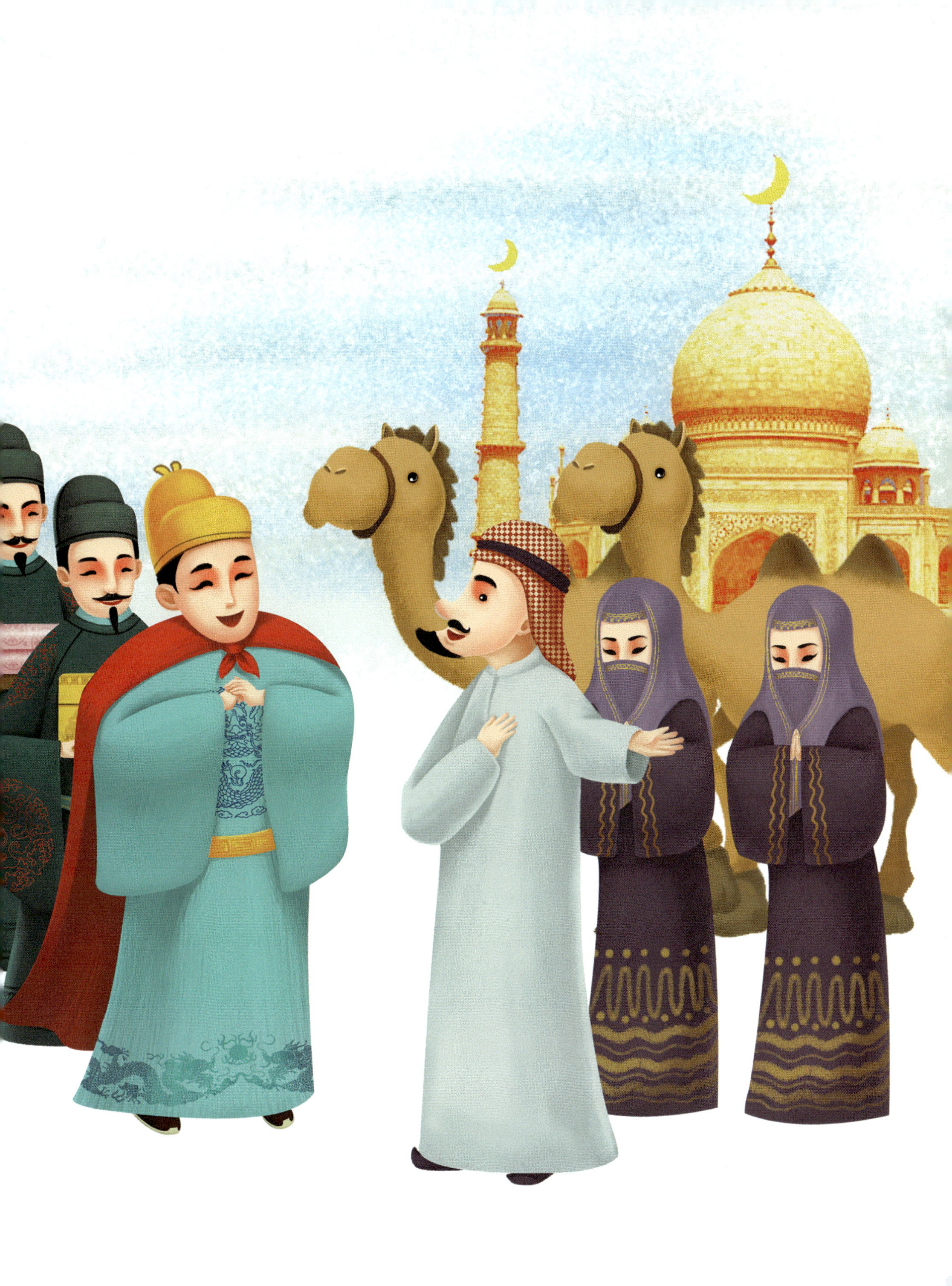

When the fleet returned to China, the emperor was delighted. 'What wonderful treasures!' he said. 'My friend, you should visit countries farther away and come back with even greater treasures.'

So Zheng He undertook six more voyages and reached as far as the Middle East and Africa, possibly even farther. Altogether, he visited more than 30 countries.

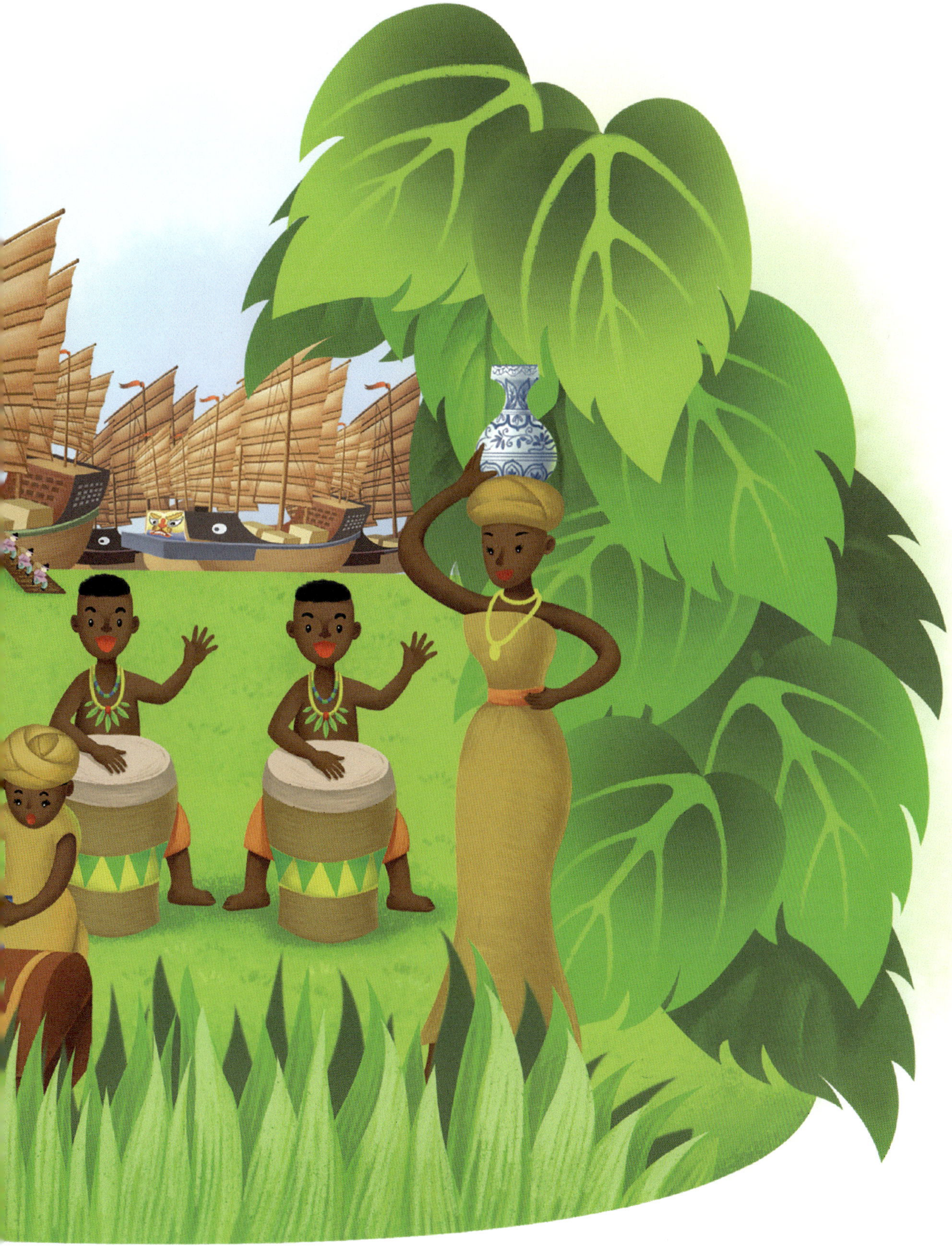

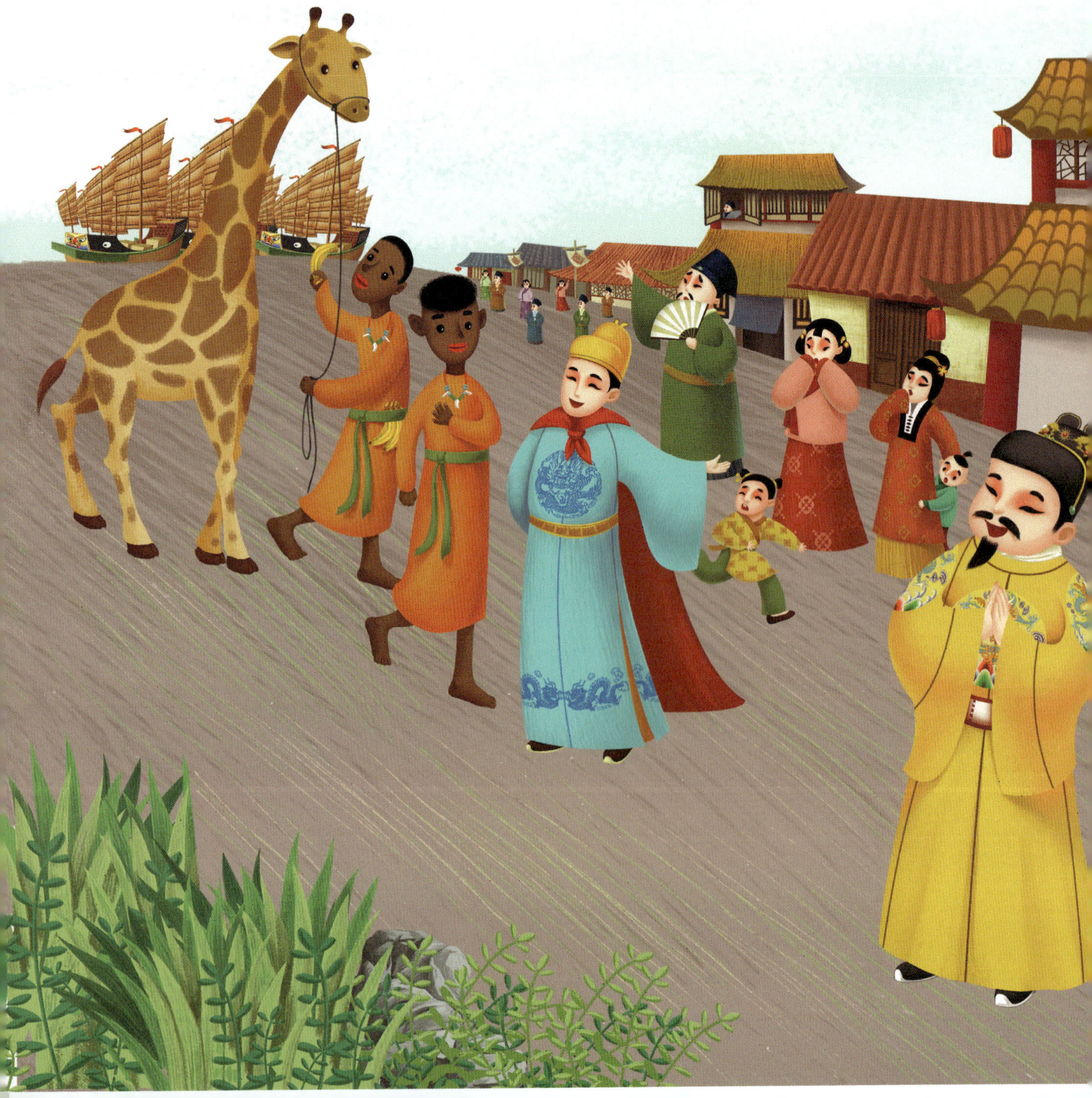

After one of his journeys, Zheng He brought back a giraffe from the African town of Malindi in today's Kenya.

When he arrived in China, people crowded the streets to catch a glimpse of the animal and the strange, dark-skinned people from far away. The Chinese thought the giraffe was a special creature called a 'qilin' (*cheelin*), which only appears when the country is doing well and the people are happy.

The giraffe and other strange-looking animals were kept in a special garden. This became the very first zoo in China.

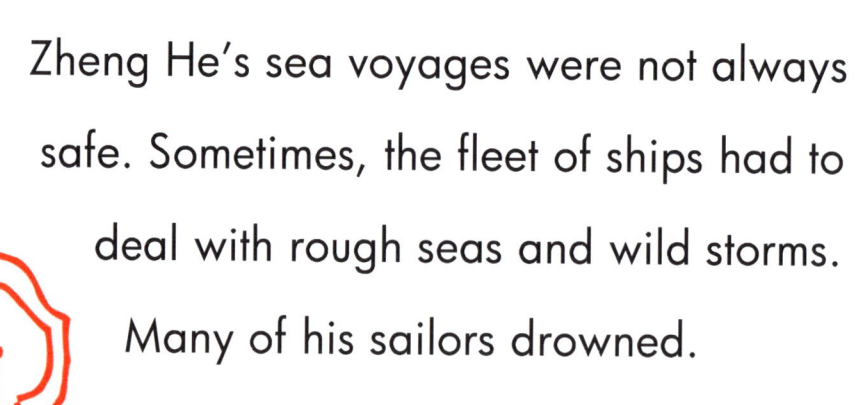

Zheng He's sea voyages were not always safe. Sometimes, the fleet of ships had to deal with rough seas and wild storms. Many of his sailors drowned.

However, the greatest danger to Zheng He and his men wasn't the weather. When they were visiting countries in southeast Asia, pirates attacked the treasure ships. They started a battle, which lasted many months. Zheng He was worried and wondered how he could ever beat the pirates.

    Then he had an idea. In the middle of the night, he got some boats to move closer to the pirate ships. When they were close enough, Zheng He gave a signal. His men started shooting flaming arrows. Soon, the pirate ships were alight and ten of them burned down. Zheng He took the pirate chief and his pirates prisoner, and brought them back to China.

The seventh voyage was Zheng He's last. He died on his way back home. After his death, China stopped exploring faraway countries. The voyages had cost a lot of money. People wondered how useful the strange items from these countries really were.

The ships of the Treasure Fleet were destroyed. Even the records and log books that Zheng He had kept, got lost and were never found again.

However, Zheng He is still remembered to this day. Every year, the Chinese celebrate his first voyage on 11 July, which is also known as China National Maritime Day. Festivals in Zheng He's honor are also held in southeast Asia, where people have built mosques and temples to remember his visits.

A little boy with a big dream had become one of the greatest explorers in the world.

The End

DID YOU KNOW?

1 ~ Zheng He was very tall compared to most other people of his time. He was around 6.5 feet (2 meters) tall and his waist was 5 feet (1.5 meters). While his cheeks and forehead were high, he had a small nose, glaring eyes, teeth that were shaped like shells, and a voice that was as loud as a bell.

2 ~ When Zheng He first started work at the palace, something horrible happened to him. He became a so-called 'eunuch'. Like all the other servants in the palace, his private parts were removed so he was no longer truly male. In the palace only the emperor could be a real man.

3 ~ The ships in Zheng He's fleet were double the size compared to any other ships at the time. It is said half the trees in southern China were cut down to build the Treasure Fleet.

A ship of the Treasure Fleet compared to the ship of Christopher Columbus, who discovered America 70 years later.

4 ~ Each treasure ship was like a city. The sailors lived on the lowest level, where they also kept the goods for trading with other countries. The kitchen, rooms for officers, and an altar for prayers were on the middle level. On the top level was an observation area to calculate the ship's location.

5 ~ The hundreds of ships in the fleet sailed in a special arrangement. The treasure ships were in the middle while the other ships sailed around them to protect them from attacks.

6 ~ When they came across bad storms, the sailors believed that evil water dragons had come for them. They would call out, 'Tianfei, sweet goddess of the sea, save us!'

    Once, a thunderstorm made the waves swell as high as mountains. Zheng was sure the end was near. But when he and his crew called out to

Tianfei, a ray of light lit up the top of the masts, and the sky was filled with brilliant colors. Within minutes, the storm died down.

Zheng He was so grateful that he built a temple in Nanjing in honor of the goddess Tianfei.

Tianfei temple in Nanjing.

7 ~ The bows of the Treasure Fleet ships were painted with dragon eyes to help the sailors 'see' where they were going.

8 ~ Ships communicated with one another using drums, flags, bells, banners, and gongs. At night, the sailors lit lanterns. If they wanted to send a message far away, they used carrier pigeons.

9 ~ After his first voyage, Zheng He helped start a school teaching foreign languages to the Chinese people. The school continued to run for many centuries.

10 ~ Zheng He's tomb is located in Nanjing, but it was found empty. People believe he probably died during the treasure fleet's last voyage, and his body was buried at sea.

TEST YOUR KNOWLEDGE!

1 Where did Zheng He get the idea of traveling to foreign countries?

a) He listened to his father and grandfather tell stories of their travels.

b) He had read a lot of books about these countries.

c) He had a lot of friends who came from overseas.

2 Why did the prince let Zheng He travel to other countries?

a) Because he wanted to attack those countries and make them part of China.

b) Because he wanted to show the people from those countries how great China was.

c) Because he wanted to find a special creature called the *qilin*.

3 What were the dangers Zheng He and his crew faced while at sea?

a) Rough seas and wild storms that caused many men to drown.

b) Pirates who attacked the ships.

c) All of the above.

4   What did Zheng He do on his visits to foreign countries?

a) He slept most of the time as he was tired from his journey.

b) He exchanged Chinese treasures like silk with special goods like gems, spices, and pearls.

c) He taught the local people how to speak Chinese.

5   After Zheng He's death, why did the Chinese stop traveling to faraway countries?

a) Because they needed the ships to wage war against neighboring countries.

b) Because the voyages had been expensive, and they didn't think the strange items from overseas were useful.

c) Because Zheng He's records and logs were burned, and no one knew where to go next.

Answers to the Quiz: 1. a / 2. b / 3. c / 4. b / 5. b

CHINA

- KUNMING (Zheng He's hometown)
- XI'AN
- BEIJING (Capital city)
- NANJING (Zheng He's cemetery)
- SHANGHAI
- HONG KONG
- TAIWAN

MING

BHUTAN, INDIA, MYANMAR, LAOS, VIETNAM, MONGOLIA, NORTH KOREA, SOUTH KOREA

PACIFIC OCEAN